Event
3.0

How Generation Υ & Z are re-shaping the events industry

Shuli Golovinski

For more information please visit our website
at www.newtonstrand.com

You can order additional copies of this book on Amazon,
Barnes & Noble or at your local books retailer.

Or contact us directly at: books@newtonstrand.com

Event 3.0

*How Generation Y & Z
are re-shaping the
events industry*

Shuli Golovinski

Foreword

Our world is changing, and a lot of people haven't even begun to notice these changes yet. While the event business is wallowing in past ideas and still doing the same things it's always done, a whole new generation has grown up wanting something different. That generation is taking over the business world, and we all have to adapt what we've been doing to their way.

Pretty soon events are going to be far different from what they've been in the past. We can either adapt to these changes or be harmed by them. We can change the world, but we also have to understand that the world will change on its own. If we work with those changes and even get ahead of the curve, we can be seen as visionaries.

Granted, no one can totally see the future, and it's always going to be uncertain. However, all of the predictions I put forward in this book are based on solid research and observation. My kids' generation is going to be ruling the world in a lot less time than I'd like to admit to myself.

As you read through this book, take time to think about how you can turn your events into something truly different and special. Life is all about evolution and change, and the changes you make could usher in a whole new way of running events. You could get the next big idea from this humble book, and take it further than I ever would've imagined.

If you do that, I would love a testimonial.

Thank you for taking the time to read this, and I hope to make every moment spent on these pages worth your time. I hope you'll learn a lot and be inspired to learn even more later on.

This book was made possible through my experiences with the people who make events happen. If this book has helped you, or if you feel that something was missing, I would love to hear from you.

Please e-mail me at Shuli@newtonstrand.com if there is any room to improve.

This book is dedicated:

To my amazing wife, who created five amazing little people I never knew I needed so much.

And to my five Generation Z's, you amaze me every day with what the human mind can adapt to. You keep me young, and sometimes you make me feel very old.

Table of Contents

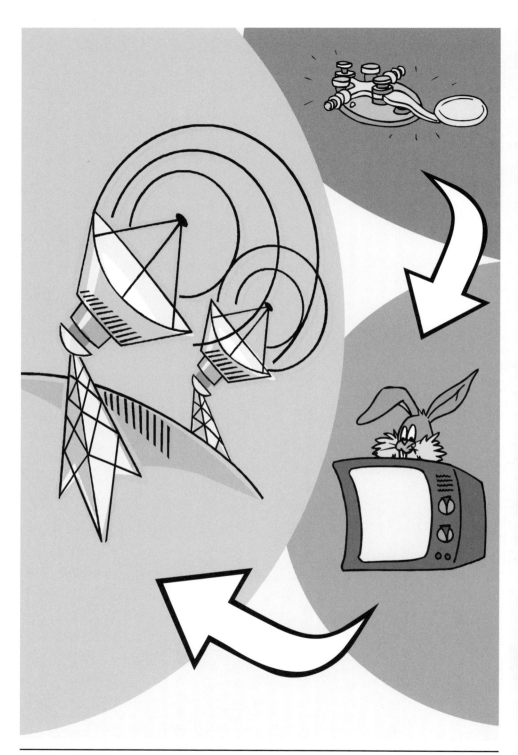

1. It's a World of Revolution...

The Internet has come a very long way since it began. While the first Internet was for the military, the Internet we all know came about in 1989. The very first website, info. cern.ch, was almost entirely made up of what the Internet can do with things such as hyperlinks. It didn't really do much, because it had nowhere to link to.

In the years that followed, the dot-com bubble began to slowly swell up as Web 1.0 formed up. With Web 1.0, the Internet was nothing more than a series of barely interactive billboards that a person could choose to read as they saw fit. The entire interaction was of that of consumer and broadcaster, and no interaction ever really occurred. While e-mail existed, this was new and obviously private.

One could even argue that an e-mail barely qualifies as part of the Internet. The Web's power back in those days was as an advertising tool and for the relaying of information. Unfortunately, it only worked in one direction, and it raised privacy concerns. But even when those concerns began to fall away, the fact remained that for several years the Internet was companies and individuals talking at people.

If you have ever talked to someone who never let you get a word in edgewise, you understand how annoying it is when someone does that regardless of what medium they use. For awhile the Internet was only attractive to people who enjoyed soaking up information, which led to the classic understanding of computer people being nothing but nerds.

As time went on, a lot of people began to create their own websites. While theories vary a lot between sources, some people have speculated that this is what caused the dot-com bubble to burst. There were too many individuals trying to pass themselves off as experts without allowing any kind of discussion to take place.

While there is certainly nothing wrong with having strong opinions and being confident about them, the entire nature of life is to have a conversation. A person needs to have their opinion be heard, and that includes when they're trying to debate their ideas against someone who boorishly declares an opinion which seems preposterous. This was among the chief factors that led the Internet to finally evolve into Web 2.0.

Web 2.0

The Web was a very one-way street from its earliest days to about 2002. At that point, Web 2.0 began to take root all over. This was a lot different from Web 1.0, but it was subtle at first. If you looked at an early website next to a Web 2.0 site, you'd probably notice that Web 1.0 relied on things like framesets.

What you most likely wouldn't notice at first would be comments sections. You also might not initially notice that a lot of these sites aren't independently hosted on a free server that lets them talk at their visitors. Most of the sites you see today are blogs or profiles of some sort. These are more than just stores you can window shop through or billboards to put propaganda into your mind. These are sites where interaction is the way things are.

While Web 1.0 was all about getting the Internet in front of people and showing them what it can do, Web 2.0 was all about figuring out what an individual person can do with the Internet. It's amazing what a person can do using only simple tools, and when the desire to do something is strong enough the results can be fantastic. The Internet has gone from being a fairly boring place full of ads and speeches to a place where speech goes every which way.

Web 2.0 saw people experimenting with blogging for the very first time. What is a blog but a place where an ordinary person can speak their mind and be heard by everyone? In reality, it's even more than a private sounding board. A blog is a place where the people can speak together, even if they're just going to bicker.

Web 2.0 has also seen the rise of social networking, which is also called social media. There is a very important difference between those two terms, a full discussion of which is beyond the scope of this book. Simply put, social media is the act of advertising in a context where people can show off their reactions to your marketing efforts. By contrast, social networking is when two or more people seek to connect and communicate through an online medium as equals.

Social networking and social media aren't always the same thing. Social networking can be spontaneous, whereas social media tends to be more planned and measured out. In time, these two ideas will merge on the Internet. If this book were about how the Net is changing, we would delve far more deeply into the nature of those two ideas. For now, let's just remember that these ideas didn't even exist during the era of Web 1.0.

Web 2.0's entire reason for existing is so that ordinary people can speak their minds and share their individual strengths with the world. Moreover, they can do so without having to also be good enough at coding and website administration to build and arrange hosting for their own sites. Anybody can simply visit a free blog hosting site, sign up and post within minutes. It takes no skill except for literacy -- and if you read some blogs, you might even consider that requirement a little less than crucial.

The point of this discussion is to state how Web 2.0 has changed the Internet. Had Facebook started in 1995, it wouldn't have likely grown very large. What would a social networking site be like if people could do nothing but look at professionally produced sites that offered little more than snapshots and billboards for whatever was being sold? It wouldn't be much of a site, and it certainly wouldn't be very popular.

The difference between Webs 1.0 and 2.0 ultimately boils down to the different ideas of authority. When a central authority figure decides what should and shouldn't be posted for all to see, it becomes a lot like classic newspapers. If an opinion isn't considered to be right by one supposedly elite individual, it's squashed before it ever sees the light of day.

When the people can decide on their own content, and respond to what other people write in an open forum, it achieves a dream no modern democracy ever has. The people get to speak their minds freely, and can agree or disagree for everyone to see. This is the most brilliant development of the last 20th and early 21st centuries. Unfortunately, this development has primarily been on the Internet, and hasn't spread to certain other areas where it could be beneficial.

The event industry has so far failed to accomplish the same sort of shift that the Internet made several years ago.

Events 1.0

If you look at most kinds of events today, you'll notice that they tend to come off looking like the Internet did in the 1990s. There are speakers who talk at the masses of people, and a steering committee has decided what the attendees should be seeing and hearing. The structure of the event comes across as thoroughly planned.

While there's nothing bad about having a plan and seeing it through, sometimes it's possible to plan too thoroughly and end up developing problems. Some of those problems are boredom in your attendees and having them not come to your next event. Ultimately, events are in the same place they were a hundred years ago, even though pretty much everything else in the world has changed a lot since then.

The average event is still a place where a central authority talks at people like a preacher on a radio show -- telling people what's right or wrong, treating their own opinions as the only way a rational person can think, and expecting an audience that just sits and listens passively. Today's audiences are far too spoiled to be passive about their information.

We'll talk in the next chapter about how today's audiences are different from those of the past. For now, let's just agree that the methods of yesterday aren't going to keep on working in the future. Events where a speaker just talks at people are the old way of the event industry, and soon enough they'll mostly be replaced by ways that are even better and a good deal newer.

If our industry is going to keep on going, we need to get out of event 1.0 thinking. This has been going on since horses and buggies were mankind's main mode of transportation. Just as we've embraced cars and ultimately computers, we also need to embrace a whole new way of looking at how we run our events. We need to think beyond event 1.0, and perhaps even past event 2.0. I have a theory on what makes up event 2.0, and why even that isn't enough for our modern audiences.

Events 2.0

The event world reaches the 2.0 level when we began to allow our audiences to speak to each other in a networking framework, as much of the industry already has. The traditional coffee break between presentations has become a more and more important part of the total package an attendee wants out of an event.

While events used to mostly be places to pick up new information on a topic of interest, that's old hat these days. Today you can just go online and research practically anything. Today networking is a far bigger deal than mere information sharing. We need to connect people to each other if our events are going to hold traction in this new age.

For most attendees, looking up information online is the way to go. But we can do a lot more than just allow people to stand around and chat with each other. We can actually make our events into something totally interactive, and work to harness the wisdom of the crowd. Together, a lot of people tend to be far wiser than a small group of people trying to account for a large number of different tastes. Let's look at the wisdom of crowds in more detail.

The Wisdom of Crowds

This concept comes from a book published in 2004 by James Surowiecki, where he argued that a large group of people can make decisions far more effectively than can an individual or a small group. In his book, Surowiecki argues that there are three major ways in which a large group of people makes the best decisions:

1. Cognition

One person's judgment tends to have far more flaws about it than does a large group's. Consider how a group's vote tends to encompass a lot more viewpoints than any one person is likely able to. A group of people thinking together can synergize solutions to problems that even a brilliant individual is unlikely to ever come up with.

2. Coordination

People are always working to fit together, since we're a social species. While where we all stand when we're taking a coffee break might not be important, how we naturally coordinate our thoughts and efforts says a lot about how much a given individual can contribute to an event's discussions. Ordinary attendees all need to have the right to speak and be listened to, because you never know who is going to steal the show by taking an idea someone else thought of and refining it into something more concise and even more thought-provoking.

3. Cooperation

Cooperation is a lot like coordination, but this is different in that it stresses building upon other people's ideas instead of merely refining them. If coordination allows people to make an idea easier to understand, cooperation is the process of adding more ideas the group can then work to understand.

Any event where people are free to chime in with their ideas is totally different from the classic model presenters tend to take. While most traditional presentations end with a question and answer session, this tends to come off as little more than an expert further showing off their expertise. In some disastrous moments, a speaker will over-extend themselves and end up saying something several members of the audience know to be incorrect. At this point the questions will either turn into an awkward silence, or an argument will erupt from the cross-examination that will inevitably take place.

If we're going to take our events to the next level and not only survive but thrive, we need to understand how wise crowds really are. Everybody has something to contribute, and if you have any doubts about that just check out YouTube. While a lot of videos are poorly made and ridiculous, almost every video makes a contribution of some kind.

If we don't take into account that our very attendees might themselves be brilliant and willing to share their wisdom, we might as well chuck our resumes and go back to school for a new profession.

2. The Generations that Craft this World...

The entire concept of different generations based on when a person was born started during the 19th century. Before that point the notion of a cultural generation had yet to be invented, and the notion of a generation referred only to the different offspring within individual families. A cultural generation is defined as a cohort of individuals born within a similar time frame who share similar cultural experiences.

Naturally a group of people born in the 1950s won't have the same cultural experience as people who were born in the 1980s, much like those same people will have vastly different general experiences than those who are being born right now. To assume that people from what are essentially different worlds should think in the same way is rather like assuming that people from two different college majors will choose the same profession.

For example, a young man may find himself being far more socially mobile than his father had been a mere twenty years or so earlier. With changes of this nature a man may flaunt his wealth at a relatively young age compared to his ancestors. As well, technology can place a massive role in changing the way a society behaves.

With new technologies come some degree of obsolescence for a previous generation's wisdom. For a generation who was raised when the average computer took up an entire room, carrying around a virtual supercomputer with access to incredible amounts of knowledge has to be a strange experience. Technology and its familiarity have shaped the most recent generations more than any others in the past.

The structure of a society can change dramatically, and two different generations may find themselves coming from dramatically different places with regard to how groups think. In the case of today's workplace and today's event industry, not two but four generations are doing their best to work together despite the vastly different ways in which each generations thinks about everything from their own careers to the world at large. Let's examine some of the differences between our current groups of generations who make the business world what it is today.

Veterans, Silent, Traditionalists

There are three subtle but distinct time periods during which the eldest group of workers were born. However, for simplicity's sake most of these individuals may be considered as having been born between the years 1922 and 1945.

Some of the oldest among this group served during World War II, and the youngest of these individuals were the children of these vets.

This generation is distinct in several ways. For one, they have a deep and abiding respect for authority. This respect means that this is a generation that has a great deal of discipline in what it does, and is the most likely generation to conform to rules and regulations. For such a person, doing what the boss says is the only way, whether the boss is right or wrong.

This makes perfect sense considering the nature of orders during war time. For a member of this generation, being told to do one thing and doing another could literally be the difference between life and death. While business instructions carry far less potential for injury or death, the same instincts carry on to everything such a person does.

For this generation education is something of a dream. Many people from this age didn't have the opportunity to get beyond the high school level, and this has lessened their career expectations over the years. A member of the veteran generation sees an educated person as deserving of a great deal of respect. This has significantly informed the way they have come to view events.

For the eldest of the current generations, an event is a means of acquiring the knowledge of an expert, which is viewed with the highest level of esteem. Since this generation was raised in a world where the best kind of distant communication was a memo or a rotary phone, using a more advanced type of technology to gain knowledge and professional insight feels foreign to them.

The work ethic of the eldest generation is also far different from the other generations in the mix. To them, working hard and sacrificing for the greater good are just what you have to do. This is a generation that respects leaders who command and control them and work by directives. While this generation works best in interpersonal interactions, they communicate best in the formal style that is in its element during a formal presentation.

The eldest current generation grew up during a time of serious deprivation. The Great Depression was an early part of this generation's experience, if not the very first part of their lives. Because of this, the eldest generation is used to scrapping it out with whatever resources they have available. While they aren't as well versed in the use of technology, their experiences have taught them that when all else fails, you have to use what you've got available.

When you want to motivate the eldest currently working generation, you want to express that theirs is a job well done and that their experience is respected. For them, no news is the best kind of news. Because of this, the most senior generation goes to events partially because their bosses tell them to, and partially because they gain knowledge best through listening to established experts. The next generation, the baby boomers, are a completely different lot.

Baby Boomers

The baby boomer generation is generally accepted to have been born between the years 1946 and 1964. Many of this group of people are the children of the vets, and the two generations almost couldn't be any more dissimilar to one another. The ways they view family, technology, work and just about everything else are often at opposite ends of the spectrum -- which is fairly common for parents and children.

To the baby boomer, their most core values are to be optimistic and to be involved. Remember that this is the generation that brought us equal rights for minorities and women and opposed a war with all their might. Of course, this is also a generation that can be very skeptical. As they've grown older their naivete has decreased, meaning that this is a generation that has gotten almost jaded about how they see the world. From "buy now, pay later" to one of the highest rates of bankruptcy in the history of the world, this generation was the first to question the value of business operations such as event attendance.

To a baby boomer, education was seen as their birthright. This is a generation that was brought up in the boom time after World War II ended, so affluence was their wayoflife. Events are therefore something they believe they deserve to attend just because they're working in a particular industry. Often this is a group that doesn't appreciate how much knowledge and how many contacts they can gain from being at an event in the first place.

When they go to an event, they take the notions of living in the moment and being accessible all the time as seriously as they always do. For a boomer, work is more than just something you do because you have to. A boomer on a mission is a man or woman possessed, and boomers are known for both their great efficiency and their intense desire to do things the right way. While boomers love to spend when they're at events, they also work extremely hard to make their money. This desire to have an exciting adventure is part of why boomers do so well at events.

While the elder generation will go to an event because their boss tells them to, for a boomer questioning authority is nothing new at all. They go to events because they know there are great people to meet and fascinating information to learn. When a boomer attends an event they're the most likely group to get to as many presentations that personally interest them as possible.

It's also plain to see that baby boomers are all about personal interaction when they communicate with someone, even in a business context. This generation is all about being team players and having as many meetings as humanly possible. This makes them a generation that loves to become more valuable to their employers.

One of the most important things to a baby boomer is to be valuable to their employer. Telling these people that they're needed and valuable motivates them to work effectively. They aren't interested in having a balance to their work and life because they work to live. A boomer is working for the most money and the best title they can earn, so they're the most likely generation to be paying rapt attention at an event.

After all, one never knows what sort of information could prove useful down the line. Since a boomer assumes that everyone else is pursuing their greatest passion in life, they give a lot of respect to the words of an expert. Boomers are the most likely people at an event to be taking notes over what's being said because they don't want to miss anything. However, this generation still counts as part of the old guard who are slowly receding from business in general, including the event industry.

Let's look at generation X.

Generation Xers

Gen X, also known as Xers, are the first of the newer guard to be a part of the business world. Born between 1965 and 1980, this generation is skeptical, fun and greatly informal by nature. For them, the business world is an extension of the independence they began to learn as the early latch key kids. While they're a cautious bunch, they have fairly well defined parameters about when they want to do business versus when they want to do their own thing.

The work life of a gen X person is a lot different than it was for previous generations. While earlier people saw their work as something they needed to do, Xers strive to eliminate the tasks they're assigned, often by automating the most routine and boring work they're assigned. They love structure and they love to contribute to building a business, but they see their work as a combination of challenge and contract. In short, it's just a job.

Xers see their leaders as just fellow employees. While boomers saw themselves as the colleagues of their bosses, an Xer sees their boss as one more person to be challenged. To Xers a challenge is a show of respect to another person's opinion. As such, they constantly challenge the people they work with.

To a generation X individual, communications should be direct and immediate. If you need to talk to someone you can just do it right now and use any kind of method you want. The only rules for such entrepreneurial individuals are that you need to make up your own rules. Remember that gen X is the group that turned the Internet from a piece of military and government technology into something that everybody can use.

A generation Xer is the type of person who will sheepishly ask for feedback on how they're doing. While most people respond reasonable well to some type of praise, to an Xer the best form of reward is to be free. Freedom comes about through a variety of methods, from starting a business that mints millionaires to keeping a solid balance between family and fun time and one's profession.

For an Xer, the events they attend allow them to meet with their fellow professionals. While learning is generally welcome since it lets you more effectively ask why something is a particular way, this is the generation that first coined the term "networking" to describe how they connect with others professionally.

This is also a generation that chooses which presentations they'll attend. For them, working is primarily a means to an end. From their educations onwards, Xers see the work they do as how to get what they want out of life. They carry this with them into being skeptical and selective in their event and presentation attendance. This was also the first recent generation to start questioning the supposed expertise of presenters.

Now that weve seen the more established generations detailed, let's examine the latest generation to enter the business world.

Generation Y

This group is known as generation Y, gen Y, millennials and echo boomers. Born between the years 1981 and 2000, they haven't all begun integrating into the business world yet. However, the ones who have become professionals have so far shown a far different set of traits from most of their predecessors.

While every generation says that the previous ones don't get it, in the case of the millennials this is more true than ever before. This is a generation that has been raised on technologies prior generations could hardly imagine. Half the millennials were born into a world with the Internet, so to them it's always existed. This is the most technologically

---

savvy generation in human history, and it's had an impact on everything this generation does.

The Internet isn't the only technology being developed while this generation was growing up. When they were born almost no one had a mobile phone. They were the first teenagers to grow up wanting their own pagers or expecting their own cell phones. Many of them didn't send a letter until they applied for college, but most of them were sending e-mails on a regular basis before they left middle school.

This is a generation that is all about realism. They want to know what's going on and they don't want to be misled or given a friendly sales pitch. This group of people wants to know what's going on and they want it to be worded enjoyably.

After all, this is a generation that's been raised in a middling time sandwiched between the recession of 1982 and the dot-com bust of 2000. During that period there were also the boom phases of the late 1980s and the mid 1990s, when affluence was commonplace. The latter period was the wealthiest time in human history for western society.

The echo boomers are also a group that is extremely confident. They aren't afraid to admit that college is huge expense for what you typically get, they earn their money to spend it immediately, and they aren't afraid to detail their entire lives -- even the really private stuff -- on their social networking platforms of choice. Many of these young people will actually post pictures of their driver's licenses, marriage certificates and other identifying information that can actually be used to steal their identities. This is an extremely open generation.

This is a very entrepreneurial generation, so the idea of being stuffed into a cubicle and ordered around isn't very appealing to them. While this is a generation of multitaskers, they're also a forward-thinking and very tolerant group in the work place and in their personal lives. They're tenacious and seek fulfillment as vigorously as boomers pursue their chosen causes. At the same time, millennials seek a balance in their work and personal lives and are only satisfied when the work they do is something meaningful.

When it comes to the event industry, the main reason a millennial will attend an event will be less about learning things. For them, knowledge is easy to find online. While a genuine expert is valuable to the most modern generation because so many online sources aren't reputable, the most important part of attending an event for a millennial is to network with the other bright and creative professionals they presume will be there.

Another part of gen Y that makes them unique among every other generation is that they are very into collaboration. They want their voices to be heard and they want to interact with people who have something to contribute. This is the generation raised on chat rooms and online forums, and they believe that anyone can be an expert. At the very least this generation accepts that anyone can contribute to a meaningful discussion regardless of their background.

Older generations often see millennials as being high strung and needy because of the way they interact with others in the work place. They want instant and frequent feedback, and they also want to be free to multitask on the dozen projects they're always working on. When this generation hits its stride the other generations will be amazed at what it can accomplish.

The most recent generations are changing the entire game.

The Game is Changing

The event industry hasn't changed much over the years. However, the people who attend events are changing rapidly. While the traditionalists and boomers certainly dominated the ranks in the past, nowadays their influence is getting smaller and smaller. For these groups of people retirement is a very short distance away.

However, the next 10 years are going to see more and more of generations X and Y taking over not only the event industry, but the business world in general. In addition to these two somewhat established groups, generation Z is slowly on the rise. While this group is still too young to be working as I write this, they will undoubtedly share many traits with the previous two generations. They will certainly be confident, direct and extraordinarily tech-savvy.

If we want to stay at the top of our game as event organizers we need to plan ahead and decide where we're going with the nature of our events. If we fall behind we won't get to work with gen Y and eventually gen Z as they strive to use their incredible abilities to their full capacity. To be truly great, we must be flexible and work with them instead of trying to impose what was onto those who are.

One of the most fundamental traits of the most recent generation of workers is how they want to really make a difference with what they do. For them, a career is more than just a paycheck and a line on their resume. Most of generation Y wants to change the world as much as they can, and really do something constructive. If we gear our events toward that end, they'll be a lot more attractive to the members of this generation.

However, if we continue to have events where we don't get to the point and we assume that they're just going to obediently sit for as long as we want them to, we're going to lose a lot of them. They may come to our events, but turnout won't grow as much as it should and overall attendee satisfaction won't be as high as we'd like it to be.

If we want the generations to all be satisfied with out events, we need to do more than tailor these events to one generation or another. We need to get the generations to work together by combining the best of every generation's mindset. We need to take the best of each generation's core values and work ethics, and meld them together.

Making the Generations Work Together

When a group of people works together great things happen. A wise person once said that no significant human accomplishment ever happened with only one person

---

working on it, and this is true in every industry working today. If you've ever gotten a group of people from the different generations together, you know how challenging it can be to get their different sets of values to cooperate together.

The good news about this is that different opinions about work and idea sharing build on a group's success. When you involve several of the different generations together, you can get far better results than you could if everyone worked the same way. This works especially well when you combine generations X and Y together. Both of these groups like to interact and work with others who have similar skills and abilities, so they gel well. When you structure your events, it's important to have open discussion forums so every generation can put its respective strengths into the mix, and everyone can benefit.

3. A New Generation of Attention Span

The world is changing rapidly for a lot of reasons. For one thing, the latest generations are developing extremely short attention spans, but not due to the classic reason of being immature. This is a group that can understand and interpret information faster than anyone who has come before them could.

One benefit of this huge amount of technological exposure is that these generations have learned how to process information at the extraordinary speed at which a computer can present it. While no human's brain works as fast as a computer can, the latest generations are so used to computers that anything presenting information slower practically puts these young people to sleep. It ultimately comes down to attention spans and how they're used.

Most events aren't built for this kind of person. The traditional form of most events stresses sitting still for a long time and being told more and more about a very small topic for 45 minutes to an hour at a time. The most recent generations are the least likely people ever to want to sit still for that long listening to such a thing, because they tend to get things far faster than the previous generations did.

For an event to really reach a person from these generations it has to be a lot faster and a lot more concise than the traditional methods have been. For them, sitting still and being talked at just isn't the most effective method of learning most things. This is a generation for whom patience isn't a virtue, but decisive action always is.

The Long and the Short of Attention Spans

An attention span is how long a person can sit still and focus on one topic or activity. While people generally develop longer attention spans as they get older, you'll generally find that everyone has a longer attention span for doing things they really want to do. A great example of this can be seen at an early age.

Give a child some free time, and they'll naturally try a bunch of different things to see what they like best. Human nature in its purest form is the simple exploration of what's interesting, and children embody this better than anyone else. Give a child some time to do whatever he likes, and he'll drift around through different activities until something really strikes his fancy. At first he'll just try things for a few minutes, until it gets old. But you'll notice when he finds something really interesting because it'll dominate his attention for a long time.

When a child finds something he enjoys doing, he can become all but obsessed with it. If you've watched a kid play with miniature cars, dolls or even marbles, you'll see that when they're free to do so, a kid can become so engrossed in something that the rest of the world seems to fall away from them entirely. As a person grows up, this doesn't change much.

As adults, we tend to race around from one task to another without really getting a chance to indulge in one for very long. There are naturally some exceptions, such as when you really an especially good book or if you write programming code. However, the tendencies of the different generations are to have different levels of attention span.

For instance, the traditionalists take pride in a job well done. For them, toiling away on anything from building a boat to composing the perfect presentation is an art form that can devour a day and be worth every second spent on it. For these kinds of people, the pace of life when they were young and the pace of life today are incredibly different. If their younger selves could've seen the way the world is today, it would've made their heads spin.

In years past, people didn't work 12 hours a day just so they could come home and work on more things before they finally collapsed of exhaustion. They worked from 9 to 5, took an hour or so for lunch, and then came home to relax and do fun things. As time goes on, it's almost like we're all trying to squeeze two or three days into each one we actually have.

With all this speed, it makes sense that each successive generation gets a little bit better at coping with and even thriving under the intense time pressures we put on ourselves. While it doesn't really have to be done today, we all pretend it does -- and that applies to everything from turning in a project all the way to doing the laundry. While the traditionalists and the baby boomers are known for having very long attention spans, generations X and Y and a whole lot faster-paced. This isn't just in their professional lives, either.

These are people who go out on Friday night and hit ten night clubs because a club can get boring in a hurry. Their social engagements are just as rapid-fire as their work lives are because they're cranked up all the time. They don't have a stop button or an off switch. It all comes down to how long a person's attention span is.

For a person with a very long attention span, spending an hour working on something is no big deal. They might lose an hour just getting ready to get to work on something. However, for a person without much of an attention span that hour should involve doing at least three or four different things. In a lot of cases such a person will be doing several things at the same time if they can.

When a person is into working quickly, they tend to show the same kinds of signs as a person who doesn't have much of an attention span. They get restless and bored very easily, and they can even become hostile if they're prevented from moving on to the next thing. To a person like that, there's always a next thing and it's always important. For a generation as fast as the millennials are, it's easy to see how they got as fast as they are.

How Fast Millennials Are

The latest generation of workers is also the fastest generation to date. They may be able to attend to a task for a lengthy period of time, but they also tend to leap from one task to another like a frog who's been given coffee. This is a group that likes to move very quickly whether they're at work or at play.

For a millennial, a conversation doesn't need to single itself out and be at the center or attention. After all, this is the group that came of age at the same time the cell phone did. For them, chatting with ten people at once while they talk on the phone and text somebody is a middling investment of their intellectual resources. If you combine all of that with composing an e-mail to another person, a millennial will feel like they're making reasonable use of their time.

A millennial is also a quick study. Keep in mind that this is the generation that doesn't even pride itself on being able to become something of an expert in any given topic in only an hour or two. For them, going online and looking up a few web pages can give them plenty of knowledge to take on almost anything is really no big deal. They don't have to become a plumber, but they can learn how to install a sink in twenty minutes.

So when they take that learning speed into their professional lives, millennials can blow the doors off the rest of us. They don't have to do a huge amount of studying to get what someone is trying to say, and they don't have to sit around for hours on end listening to a lengthy lecture. This can make them a little antsy in school, and it definitely has an impact on the event industry.

See, a person's attention span isn't just about how long a person is interested in a topic or activity. It also relates to how easily the person gets a particular point, or how long they're willing to mentally engage with a topic. This can often come down to the types of research a person is used to doing, and this is where millennials differ from any previous generation.

For example, when a veteran or a baby boomer wants to learn something they'll typically ask someone about it. In a lot of cases this can turn into a lengthy meeting, which is fine because that's what this generation enjoys doing. For them, their options regarding research have always been to either talk to an expert or to pore over books where it could take hours just to find the most basic points, to say nothing about the more advanced topics.

Millennials are a whole different breed, though. To them, a topic doesn't need a lengthy discussion, and most topics don't even need to be brought to any kind of expert. While an older person would likely go to their doctor if something felt wrong with them, a millennial is more likely to just go to WebMD or some other medical site and self-diagnose whatever's wrong. In some cases they might even self-medicate.

While schools continue to operate the same way they have for decades, millennials may end up changing the way education is presented one day. This isn't a generation that wants to sit around listening to endless lectures. These people want to participate in the discussion and really contribute something to the group's learning if they can. They also want to hear what everyone else knows, even if they can't be traditionally called an expert.

The millennials know something that the rest of us still have to learn -- that being an expert is about what you really know about a subject and not just how many degrees you have hanging on your wall. For a millennial if you've got something to contribute you should be allowed to speak, even during a meeting.

This is precisely the lesson we need to take to heart in the event industry. While we continue to have presentations where people just sit around for hours at a time, generation Y gets the message long before the presenter stops talking and asks for questions. Keep in mind that this generation is as fast at listening as they are at reading, so they get the message long before the hour is up.

Generally, people from the millennial generation get the gist of the topic by about the fourth slide, and therein lies the problem. What happens when a person understands what you're saying about 5 minutes into your 45-minute presentation? They aren't just going to passively sit there and slowly be lulled to sleep by you constantly repeating ideas they got half an hour ago. They're going to sit there and play games or text their friends.

This is a generation that isn't going to just sit there during a presentation. They want to interact and they want to move on to new topics as they get the message. For this generation the old ways of presenting information just aren't good enough. So we have to adapt not only our messages to this new type of audience, but also the way we present these messages to them in the first place. If we don't, we're going to turn them off, and this will lead them to being less likely to return to our events.

While millennials will grin and bear it if we keep on doing things the way they've always been done, the point is to create events that they'll adore attending and champ at the bit to attend in the future. We don't want them to dread coming to our events, and to call them boring. This is why we need to get with the times and present to them in a way that works with how fast they are at learning things.

Gen Z May be Even Faster

If you thought generation Y was fast, generation Z might just make your head spin. While they're still young as I write, this generation is a group so fast and so tech-savvy that they might one day want to have computers implanted directly into their brains so they can be online constantly. If they continue the trend that generation X started and gen Y continued, they're bound to be the fastest learners ever.

Just think that a couple of decades ago nobody really knew what to do with the Internet. Generation Z knows what to do with it by the time they're old enough to walk. The Internet is a lot older than they are, and they can't even imagine a world where you can't get online. Consider the power of that statement.

Generation Z can't imagine a world without the Internet. This is their life.

This is the generation for whom googling a topic they want to learn about is as natural as brushing their teeth to clean up and stay healthy. This is a generation that knows how to use wikipedia by the time they're old enough to read. They'd need to use it to find the difference between the glossary and the index of a book.

But this is fine, because books are horribly slow. For a gen Z person the old way of thumbing through a book sounds about as quick and efficient as walking around the world trying to manually find the answer to a question or doing a long-term anthropological study. This is a generation that lives and breathes speed, and we have to respect this.

If you understand how fast gen Y is, you undoubtedly have a great deal of respect for the abilities gen Z is beginning to develop. When they start working in about ten years they're going to do things we can barely imagine today. Their ability to gather information is great, but the speed at which they attack things is even more amazing.

This is a group of young people who are used to being able to find just about anything in under a minute of their time. When they start to apply their ability to work quickly and multitask to the working world, everybody else is going to have to work twice as hard just to keep up. When gen Z hits their stride you're going to learn the meaning of "If you can't beat 'em, join 'em."

This is a generation that works with multitasking on a daily basis, even if they're too young to understand what that even is. When a person multitasks they can get even more done than if they were just doing one thing quickly the way gen Y does. Let's take a closer look at multitasking and how it's applied in ever-greater amounts by the past few generations. The way they do this is so natural that it's barely even noticeable to them.

Generation X arguably invented the idea of multitasking when computers became essential to the workplace. However, as time has gone on technology has gotten more and more essential to society outside the workplace as well. Today you'd be hard-pressed to find almost anyone who doesn't have a personal music device, a smart phone, at least one kind of portable computer and wifi in their home or office.

Consider that generations Y and Z are born into this world. For gen Y they often had cell phones before they were out of high school, and they usually had a computer in their home before they were out of middle school. Even the oldest members of generation Y began learning how to use the older Apple II types of computers in elementary school. In contrast to this, gen X and their predecessors used typewriters until at least college unless they were rich. Some traditionalists still don't have even have computers and such.

In order words, this is a whole different type of generation when it comes to how comfortable they are with using technology. For them, technology is what gives any project the power to get done, even if it's just arranging a get-together on their social networking site of choice. And it's this level of speed and connectedness that makes multitasking such a basic part of the current generation's lives. They multitask all the time and don't even think about it.

This has gotten into everything the most recent generations do. For them, sitting around and writing something feels boring and empty. There have actually been studies done that found a sort of withdrawal occurs when people who are used to texting and being online are deprived of these abilities for awhile. They seriously develop symptoms akin to the symptoms a drug addict feels when they don't have access to their drug of choice.

When the most recent generations sit around, they're not just talking. They're downloading files, texting people periodically, and even searching for tickets or random bits of trivia they're curious about. In a lot of cases they're actually carrying on two or three conversations with people they're physically next to, instead of just having a more traditional group discussion.

When you count texting, a person from the more recent generations might be carrying on a dozen conversations at the same time. This is while they're listening to music, studying and considering what's next on their agenda. So multitasking has gotten to the point where it isn't dependant on technology, but is just the way these people run their entire lives.

When a person who carries this mindset goes to any kind of event, they're not thinking in terms of just sitting around and listening to a presenter. They're actually working on their projects, texting their friends and colleagues, and even surfing the Internet looking for more information on topics they just heard about a few seconds ago. All of this is happening when gen Y is in any given presentation, because this is how quickly they can take in and process the information they're presented with.

Generation Y doesn't need to sit there for half an hour to get the point of a presentation. They can get the point of a presentation in just a few minutes, and then be tweeting their newfound revelations to their followers a moment later. While earlier generations may have needed more time to pick up a topic's gist, this generation is really on the ball about such things. They can get the basic points within a minute or two, and do their own research right there with their smart phones while the sixth or seventh slide is still walking through the basics. The interesting part is, while this is going on a gen Y individual can also still be listening.

They can both listen and do their research at the same time. This is a generation who won't just sit around doing one thing while a presenter continues to run through the basics, though. For this generation, time is the most valuable asset of all and a long attention span is more of a liability than an asset.

The Multitasker's Attention Span

For people in generations Y and Z, it doesn't take a long time to do much of anything. While these people can appreciate that sometimes getting things done takes awhile, they understand how precious time is. For them, having a long attention span and a lot of patience tends to slow down projects that can make a serious impact.

Previous generations were used to having to call someone sometimes several times and wait until they were at home to arrange a meeting, today's young people are used to sending a text or two and meeting their quarry immediately. While previous generations had to either meet in person or send a letter if they wanted to get across something more detailed than a phone call could express, for today's young people an e-mail isn't even the simplest way to get such a detailed message across.

Keep in mind that this is a generation who is used to communicating in 140 characters or less through Twitter. While this is great, the most important part of this involves how easily this generation interprets the ideas you can present in 140 characters or less. For these young people, reading something tends to mean rapidly absorbing it and working with it immediately instead of having to wade through a massive book to gain understanding.

Today's generations aren't interested in settling down into doing just one task. When they work, they're always open to communications from whomever might be interested in giving them a project or a valuable piece of insight. Even when the most recent generations are at play, they're talking, typing and checking out the area even while they're running around in the game trying to cut down their opponents.

For those of us involved in creating the events this generation is starting to go to, we can use this tendency to multitask to our advantage instead of letting it hinder us. If we let it get in our way we'll just end up alienating the youngest generations and ultimately harming ourselves in the process.

Remember that this is the generation of the instant guru.

Event 3.0

4. The Instant Guru...

There was a time when people went to events, not so much to network with other professionals in their industry, but to learn important information about how to do their jobs more effectively. While this will never completely go out of style, the fact of the matter is that more and more people are going to events for "face time," or the kind of networking that only happens in person. This kind of networking is crucial for the emerging millennial generation, who do most of their networking online.

While it's easy to see how many social networking sites there are nowadays, the number of these kinds of websites doesn't even tell half the story. While it's obvious that a lot of people just want to put up a page that tells something about themselves and invites other people to contact them, a lot of more ambitious people want to go the extra mile and become the newest type of stars and gurus.

The most modern generation has gone in a direction almost no one could have imagined only a few years ago. In the same way the Internet changed so many things and

Web. 2.0 rocked the world, today's generation is rocking it in yet another way through de-emphasizing the classical guru that used to be venerated all throughout society and especially during presentations.

While ours is a species that will always celebrate the contributions of exceptional people, the way we're doing so is far different than it used to be. While in the past the exceptional people needed to network with someone who was already established and powerful, today being acknowledged as being great just means doing it and putting it up online.

Generation X used to be the most intensely connected generation going. However, they've since surrendered that title to the millennials, who are very quickly going to need to duke it out with gen Z to see who can be the most connected of all. While it might seem like connections are just a natural part of the human experience, for a lot of people this isn't the case at all. For some, connections come about primarily because of who they meet online.

In the same vein, famous people in this day and age aren't discovered by some kind of talent agent and put on some kind of track to becoming popular and well known. Some of the biggest stars going today started out with nothing more than the desire to get somewhere and the drive to do something about it. Couple that with being able to put yourself online and be seen and the next thing you know, anybody can be famous.

This more open and accepting road to fame is better than we've ever seen before in this world. Not only does it allow people with large egos to see themselves and be talked about, but it also allows a lot of great ideas to get out there. In this day and age a common, ordinary person who has some great ideas can become something of a guru. The crazy part is that it takes little more than a video camera, a story to share and the will to post some things to become an everyday guru for the common people.

Through posting some things online, as simple as that is, an ordinary person can put a substantial scratch on the universe. No longer do you have to go door to door campaigning to make something happen. Nowadays you can do it via the Internet, on sites like YouTube and Facebook. From those humble platforms and simple beginnings, you can move proverbial mountains with what you have to say.

It's in this type of climate that we start a whole new world of event planning and execution. Whereas at one point events were all about passing out information from major, official sources, now that entire way of thinking has been shown to be bogus. Today's young people want to do a lot more than just sit there and be talked at, especially if they feel they've got something to add to the topic being discussed.

This chapter is about the discussion that's taking place every day, all around the world. We're also going to do discuss what we as event organizers need to do to not only roll with this new way of thinking but make it mutually profitable for everyone involved in our events. If we do well, we can change how our entire industry works for the better by providing a whole lot more value than we used to.

The Generation of Connections

Connecting to other human beings has been a part of our mutual nature since the beginning of the human race. In the old days this was a very difficult process, since people live all over the world and traveling used to be extremely difficult in the days before airplane travel. As time went on, it became a lot easier to travel around and people began to share the insights they'd gained from doing their various types of work. This was the beginning of events as we know them today, just in simpler and less official forms.

With more time came all new types of events that were designed to share increasingly focused types of knowledge. One year it might have been a meeting about electronic wonders, whereas the next year it became about light bulbs and their power supplies. With still another year it became more about incandescent light bulbs, the alternating currents that power them and how to be safe while using and installing these marvelous technologies. Each year brought newer and more detailed insights into how a person could work more effectively.

In those days, the connection was mostly about connecting on thought to another by sharing information and experience. Back then networking across long distances usually took a back seat to just sharing thoughts and stories with like-minded people. The term "networking" hadn't even been invented yet, after all. So it made sense that people generally just went into presentations looking to scoop up some of the knowledge dispensed by the established, recognized experts in any given field like disciples around a guru.

However, everything changes if enough time goes by. Connections are the kind of thing that tend to change their natures every so often. Rather like parents and children eventually come to recognize one another as equals, the event industry is beginning to recognize that one doesn't necessarily need to have a particular kind of degree of amount of experience to be respectable as an equal contributor to a topic. In this day and age, a lot of the connections in the event industry aren't just between what you used to know and what you're learning right now, but between yourself and the people you're getting to know now.

Networking as a term was coined by generation Xers who were describing how they met up with and conducted business with people who could potentially help their careers down the line. In a lot of cases it just meant having brief conversations and exchanging business cards with a bunch of people you'd never speak to again. But on those rare occasions when someone you'd met at an event, while waiting for a plane, or even while you were out running errands turned into a valuable contact, it was worth all the effort you put in.

Most events these days aren't about just receiving information from an established expert like they used to be. Although this still plays a role in many types of events, a much larger part for the most recent generations of workers is about networking with other professionals. How many times have two or three people met up, struck up a conversation that got into great details and proved enlightening, and then ended up starting a business together based on what they discussed?

Connections between professionals are considered a lot more important because individuals are becoming more respected as people who deserve a level of admiration for what they bring to the table. No longer are only established experts bringing in attendees who'll sit there and passively listen to what's being said. The attendees themselves are making the most of the traditional coffee breaks in between presentations to get to know other people and share insights in a less formal capacity than the presentations.

This generation has proven to itself that a person's credentials and their credibility aren't necessarily the same thing. This is the era of YouTube stars, who have made names for themslves without all kinds of fancy degrees or being discovered in an official sense. These days a person can be discovered by other people, and have that be their way to fame and notoriety.

The YouTube Stars

If you've ever heard of Kimbo Slice and Justin Bieber, you're aware that a lot of people have made their names on YouTube and similar sites. And it wasn't just the fact that they have talent that took them to the level above local notoriety. It was also the fact that their work ethics and desires for higher levels of fame made them do something special.

Of course, in this world it isn't too special to put up some videos or write a blog to get better known. But how many people were doing things like that ten years ago? Not very many. Twenty years ago things like that were the obscure realm of public access television and writing books, both of which have an editorial element about them. In the past, people used to have to run their ideas by official authorities and be sanctioned in order to get their ideas and names out.

Today, anybody who has some fairly basic equipment can post a blog, even if they can only do so from a public library or a friend's house. And if they have a video camera with a mic (which often only costs $10 or so), they can make all kinds of videos to show off some talent or knowledge they may have. While some people choose to do something that shows off their knowledge, a lot of people just like to clown around.

Such individuals may just be messing around, but their power in a world this connected is easy to underestimate. A person who is famous or infamous can command a lot of power in certain communities, if only to ask their followers to buy or boycott a particular thing. When it comes to being a YouTube star, there are all different types. Some of these people are good fighters, while some others are good musicians or poets. Still others among this group are just folks who have a different way of looking at the world as a whole and like to share that way with others.

We live in a world where a person doesn't need to pay to get noticed like someone years ago could have. They don't need to buy space on a billboard or on TV, and they don't even need to own a computer or server and put up a dedicated website. Anybody can sign up for a blog in just a few minutes and begin making a mark on things. Anybody can post a few videos and turn themselves into a minor celebrity almost overnight.

A person can even become a common guru.

The Common Guru

While some people use their online celebrity status just to clown around, some other people prefer to use their fame to do more than just show people a good time. These people might not be gurus in the traditional, socially approved of sense, but they can still offer a lot of valuable information and thoughts to the people who watch, listen to or read what they have to say. While previous generations didn't have this much access to methods of sharing their knowledge, nowadays this is the common practice.

To become a guru, all a person really needs to do is open up an account with a blog hosting service and start writing. From there they can choose to do all sorts of technical things which aren't important to our discussion here, but that isn't the big deal. The big deal is that they have to write something of interest. It doesn't matter how many degrees they have, even if this number is none at all. It doesn't matter how much experience they have at anything. Sometimes very young people can utter brilliant, thought-provoking statements that end up turning the world on its ear.

The only common factor involved in being a common, everyday guru is that you have to say something that people listen to. Your message has to resonate with others and be repeated and appreciated. While a great message is generally shared, it doesn't have to be. It just has to reach someone and have a profound impact on that other person's life. Isn't that the ultimate definition of what a guru is?

The common gurus come in all shapes, sizes, colors and genders. There is no benefit to being part of a particular group when you have something intelligent to contribute. You just need to find a way to get that message out, and someone will find it. If it really resonates well, more people will come around and tag it as they see fit. If it goes viral and gets linked to and talked about like crazy, you might end up becoming an Internet celebrity, but there's no harm done if it doesn't.

For a common guru, the fame isn't really the important part. True, some of these gurus are out to sell books, audio courses, videos, merchandise or what have you, but that's just their business. When it comes right down to it, these are people who are trying to get a message out to the rest of the world and have their thoughts and opinions matter. A thought that just bounces around in someone's head is ultimately pretty useless to anyone but an idle dreamer.

This is why the millennials are so interested in networking, as opposed to receiving information from a presenter at an event. In a lot of cases they can find the same information at any time just by going online, without having to hear it repeated several times and explained from several different angles. In a presentation it makes sense to be a little redundant because traditionally this might be the only time a member of the audience might hear a particular piece of information. However, it makes very little sense in this modern era.

Today an attendee can pull up the same info they're receiving from the presenter, not just on their computer back in their hotel room but on their smart phone right then and there. Sometimes the information is even delivered in a more interesting and thought-provoking manner by a common guru on YouTube than by this highly esteemed, heavily degreed, possibly quite boring and professorial presenter.

And in some cases, one or more of the attendees might themselves be common gurus, and be looking to augment their already impressive levels of knowledge on the topic at hand by attending an event in the first place. If all the information they can get at an event is just the same old stuff they already know, it can be very disappointing for them. One of the worst things is already knowing what the presenter is saying as he says it. Another of the worst things is knowing that you won't be hearing anything you don't already know for the better part of an hour.

The process of a common guru's development is a lot different from that of a traditional guru. While at one point being in a position to hand out information meant you were somehow respected by your colleagues, nowadays it just means you personally believe you've got something to say that's worth listening to. In the past, presenters were generally selected by a steering committee or other group who had heard of them and respected their past work. However, today that makes a lot less sense than it used to.

In years past, the people who gave our society its information had to go through some kind of formal approval process in order to be seen and heard. Whether there was purchasing time and navigating the FCC's rules, impressing a committee of some sort or getting a job which allowed you to get up in front of a significant audience, being respected was as much a matter of who you knew as what you knew. If you wanted to get your message out, you often had to change it to fit what someone else thought the people should see and hear. Censorship is practically guaranteed under a system like that.

However, a common guru doesn't have to think in terms of what sponsors and bosses think about what they have to say. They can just let slide whatever's on their minds, even if it's rough and profanity-laden, and people will get the unvarnished story in the guru's own words. Contrary to what many people think about offending the public, this candor is often appreciated by the people who respect what the common guru has to say.

Becoming a common guru is in some ways easy and in some ways difficult.

Becoming a Guru

Being the kind of person whose thoughts and opinions other people respect is both easy and hard. As the saying goes, it's easy to do but hard to do well. Garnering respect has always been a challenge to people who carry such lofty goals. For them, it isn't about having someone pushing at their backside and driving them onward. People who strive to be famous or to just get their message out there are the types of self-starters who don't need someone sitting on their shoulders with a riding crop, and they don't need a drill sergeant shouting at them to crank out one more video or blog post.

Allowing our attendees to become gurus at our events through allowing them to be short-duration presenters in the Chance2Speak style. When we give a lot of people who aren't professionals but do have insights to share a chance to do so, we won't know what kind of event we'll have until the end. But it'll certainly be exciting in its unpredictability, and it'll definitely involve a lot of ideas that having one presenter speaking for 45 minutes wouldn't touch on.

We might even make a scratch on the universe...

Scratching the Universe

Everybody wants to make their mark on the world and make a scratch on the universe. There are a lot of ways to do this, and more ways are being invented every day. The most easy ways to really make a mark are to get people involved in what you're saying and to get them to help you make things happen in the real world. This is the message that most people from gen Y carry with them subliminally, much the same way that the traditionalists carry the message of work hard and you'll be prosperous.

When your attendees strive to make their individual scratches on the universe, you should help them to do this. You need to give them all as many tools as you can to let their voices be heard, and to meet the people who will help them make their dreams and ideas into reality. When the right people meet, an amazing thing called synergy happens. It's where several people work together in a spirit of trust and mutual respect, and it allows people to think up ideas better than any one of them ever could have created.

So let's close this chapter with some ideas to make your events conducive to making this happen.

Carving Out New Events

Today's events need to change a lot if we're going to make the most of what the most recent generations have to offer the world. While we can always keep on doing the same old things, that's just not the best strategy anymore. In this world, putting an established expert in place to present their knowledge for 45 minutes to an hour just doesn't allow the most information to get spread. In some cases it isn't even the best information possible.

As event organizers we need to allow the young people who have a lot to contribute to our events to do so as much as possible. After all, this is a generation that has a lot to offer one another, both in fellowship and in the sharing of their individual knowledge. When one millennial learns something, they're bound to share it through their blog or videos anyway. What we can do is take what they're already doing naturally and unofficially, and make it into something more official.

When we present a forum where a group of people can each speak their piece, a lot of information can be shared between these people. This way a lot of learning can happen, and more importantly great things can get done from a networking perspective. These are what our attendees want the most nowadays.

Making Use of New Technologies

Putting together more interactive exhibitions is a major part of bridging the gap between the most recent generations and the previous ones. However, this is nowhere near the entire story. We also need to make technology a more central component of our shows if we're going to court today's youngest attendees.

Technology is a major part of their lives, after all. These are kids who grew up with the Internet in their rooms. Their high school days featured cell phones, and they were expected to type everything. It's gotten to the point where handwriting isn't even taught anymore. If we want to share our insights with newer generations, we have to keep technology as a significant part of the event-going experience.

Some event organizers haven't been quick to embrace the new technologies available to us. Being on the cusp of the latest technologies means a whole lot more than just putting a bar code on the back of every attendee's name tag. In a world where everybody is connected to everybody else, we need to keep an open mind on technology and let it help us every way it can.

A great example of this is social networking. If your event's website doesn't have an option to allow your attendees to network with each other and set up meetings easily, you're missing out on one of the most powerful functions your events have. Why settle for letting your attendees meet at random when you can be proactive in helping them find others?

The more your events' technology helps your attendees to network effectively, the better your events will be known as the places to be. Budgets are tight, and some people today wonder why an event is so important. Today's attendees don't need to go to an event to learn the latest news and wisdom in their various professions. They can look up just about anything online.

So let's help them find what they need. As we talked about earlier, some of the best information isn't found in a book or even on YouTube. It's found straight out of an expert's mouth. Experts are still a major draw of events, and the chance to exchange knowledge with an expert in-person is often priceless.

Structured networking is an efficient way for attendees to meet one another. But when an attendee wants to have a great conversation with a presenter, their options used to be limited. Nowadays, that limitation no longer applies. Attendees don't have to just hang around after a presentation and hope they can snag the presenter for a moment or two. They can introduce themselves beforehand and meet the presenter after their speech using a pre-planned meeting.

Using a service like Chance2Ask, an attendee can do this during the presentation and actually alter the direction the speaker ends up taking. People aren't videos, after all. We can go from one topic into another one if someone has a great question for us. When a person poses a great question, it can start all kinds of additional conversations.

These are the chief ways we can give our attendees what they want the most.

In the next chapter we'll expand on what they want a little bit more.

5. What Attendees Want Today

Attending an event isn't what it used to be. We can do so many things technologically that we couldn't before, but technology is just the tools we use. The people who attend events in this day and age are a whole different group from the old days. We have to work with a whole new way of thinking about who our attendees are and what they want.

One thing our attendees want is to be understood. Naturally everybody wants to be understood and to have their concerns matter to other people. But with today's youngest generations, this is even more important than it ever was before. Keep in mind that the millennials don't just want constant feedback, they demand it.

Another thing the newest generations want from the events we organize is real expertise. One of the worst parts about having a world in which everyone can be a guru is that there is a very low ratio of real experts to people who just pretend they know what they're talking about.

Real expertise is a seriously prized and unfortunately rare commodity in this day and age.

Of course, real expertise isn't the only thing most attendees are looking for these days. When you find a reliable expert you can usually find their most commonly available information on YouTube, if not on their personal websites. A lot of the most recent generation's attendees like to check out events and really talk to the presenters, so they can find out the more underground information that they can't just find anywhere.

Naturally, networking is a major goal of every recent generation. As the world has gotten smaller and smaller, a person's network has gotten more and more important to making a more successful career. A great network starts with great people, after all, and why not meet them at an event where shared interests are the main topics being discussed. Round table discussions and open debates are equally great ways to get in an expert's head and remember why you respect them so much.

Keep in mind that a real expert isn't necessarily someone with a lot of degrees

Being understood and being heard are not the same thing. While being understood is very important, sometimes an attendee just wants to get his or her views and insights out there. Sometimes a person needs to share what they've worked so hard to learn, or the result is a lot of unnecessary dissatisfaction. When our attendees get to speak and be heard, they tend to be a whole lot more satisfied with their event-going experience than they would be otherwise.

On the whole, how we relate to our attendees and structure our events has got to change. We need to be more attentive to how they actually think if we're going to keep them satisfied with the events they pay good money to attend. If we ignore their interests, we'll be short-changing them and ourselves. So let's start out with understanding our attendees and branch out from there.

Being Understood

Our attendees want us to understand what they need. We touched on those needs in the opening section of this chapter, but the idea bears some repeating. In order to understand our attendees, we need to think as they think. This can require us to adjust how we think a lot.

To understand our attendees we need to drop some of our old thoughts about how an event "should" be. If we focus too much on doing things the way that's been working for a long time, we'll usually just end up rehashing the same old stale ways to run an event. If we don't do anything differently, we'll get boring, and this is a generation that doesn't take very kindly to being bored.

The millennials may just be gathering steam to really make their mark on the world, but they've already established that they're not going to take a lot of the same old stuff. They want to get somewhere and do something in this world, and they're not going to just fall in line the way their parents and grandparents would. They expect to contribute something to every event they attend, and we can forget that at our own peril.

A major part of being understood involves finding people who are kindred spirits. While that might sound a little informal, remember that this is a generation that somewhat takes after the gen Xers in having a very forthright type of informalness about them. When this group gets together, they aren't all business. And when they do talk business with one another, they generally like to talk with people who are similar to themselves in some ways.

The kind of understanding a lot of millennials desire also comes from having shared experiences to relate with among themselves. Personality types can work well together in all sorts of predictable ways, especially if they have some common experiences to bind them together. This is the ultimate angle that turns an event into something greater than just getting a bunch of people into one room and having them learn things. Learning is great, and it should definitely be a part of every event, but a lot of this learning needs to be done between people.

In an event where people start really understanding others and being understood themselves, a great thing happens among your attendees. They start to understand more than what they could if they were receiving some kind of "one size fits all" message. Remember that this is a generation that has been bombarded with advertising since before it was even born. They're very sensitive to the generic corporate sales pitch, so don't even try.

You need to show your attendees at every age group that you are willing to make the effort to understand who they are, how they formed mentally and what they want. Showing this means structuring your events in ways that allow your attendees to interact with each other and share their knowledge in the best ways they can. Often this is a generation that has to limit how well it's understood to how much they can share with other people online, and that will never be as complete as it can be in person.

You also need to keep in mind that this is a generation that shares obsessively. When a person in the millennial generation has a major life event, they're sharing it with people on their Facebook and Twitter accounts before they talk to anybody else in the room with them about it. This might seem strange, but in a lot of ways it makes sense to share that way first. In order to understand this generation a bit better, let's talk about why they tend to speak with people online before others in person.

In person, things tend to be a lot more off the cuff. When a person feels something very emotional, they might not be able to make it look or sound good. Even in a state of serious emotional turmoil, and especially during more normal times, this generation is as image conscious as any other has ever been. In most ways they're even more obsessed with their images because they can easily be found and communicated with anywhere they might go.

When a millennial goes online first, they can clear up their thoughts and make them a bit more coherent than they could when they're just talking in the moment. When

---

a moment comes on, especially when it's a moment that's charged up with a lot of feelings, even the most composed and eloquent person can feel really hard pressed for the right words. This is one of the hardest things to take about being misunderstood- when you know precisely how you're feeling and what you want to say, but for the life of you it just won't come out properly.

Of course, being understood goes beyond just sharing some past experiences. Some events are organized with gimmicks to link people together through having joined and united current experiences around each other. But beyond all the silly gimmicks, a lot of things can be said for finding the shared experiences of a group of people and tapping into them for your events. We'll discuss the more practical applications of this in the next chapter.

Being understood also extends into the realm of being able to learn in one's own fashion. Remember that the millennials are a group who are used to having everything be customized just for them. When you provide them with all kinds of options for how to learn, such as group and panel discussions and presentations where anyone is able to ask or directly text in questions, you can help them to learn far more effectively than if you only supplied one type of presentation in your events and asked the attendees to adapt to that.

One of the best ways to help your attendees to be understood is to help them find real experts to talk to. When you do this, you'll often find that the process of understanding doesn't need to be tailored nearly as much.

In a lot of cases it ends up tailoring itself as people talk amongst themselves naturally. A good presenter isn't a video, and they can talk as candidly as anybody else can.

Finding Real Expertise

In this day and age, real expertise is a little hard to find. If you ever do a search for a topic that is a little less mainstream, you'll undoubtedly find a lot of people who sound about as coherent as drunks in a tavern babbling out their two cents worth about it. While it can be entertaining to read some of the crazy talk some people offer up, it can also be bothersome if you want to find some genuinely good information.

Keep in mind that this is the YouTube generation, and that means a lot of different things. For one, it means that these are people used to having all kinds of information available and delivered by a human being on video at any time they want it. Also, this generation tends to find a lot of results when they search for any kind of information they want to find. Also, a lot of that information is not especially reliable or very well delivered, so it sometimes requires some sifting around to really find the good stuff.

Unfortunately, a lot of the information leaves a little to be desired, if not a lot. Often times you'll find that the people who create videos either don't know very much about the topics they're talking about or don't know a whole lot about making coherent videos. Finding people in YouTube videos who have practiced what they're going to say is sometimes very challenging, and this can contribute to

---

a lot of frustration as a person weeds through endless badly produced videos crafted by amateurs.

Another problem people tend to run into when they search for information these days isn't a lack of it but a huge glut of it. If you do a search for anything and get less than a hundred thousand results, it's probably a topic so obscure that most people have never even heard of it before. Today's young people are able to find just about anything, but that doesn't mean the information is necessarily that solid.

The irony about having an entire world full of people who can all post whatever they like is that most of the time nobody checks anybody else's work. Any person can just go online, post anything they dream up, and have it turn into accepted knowledge within a fairly short time if nobody bothers to check out whether it's for real. In the case of some kinds of information like laws, history or safety precautions, this can be downright dangerous.

This leads into why many young people are so ravenous to find solid sources of information. They don't want to have to wade through ten million different people's crazy opinions. They want to talk to someone who's studied the topic at great length and knows what's really up. They want to be able to confirm their suspicions on some things and be informed when they're wrong. As the old saying goes, if you ask you're a fool for a minute or two, but if you don't ask you'll be a fool for life. Millennials pride themselves on never being anybody's fool.

Of course, speaking with a real living expert isn't just about learning whether the information they found online the other day is real or fake. Mere confirmation is just a matter of looking around for awhile and determining what seems the most plausible. A lot of times there is better information that a speaker most likely wouldn't share online for everyone to see. Some information is just too good to give away flippantly.

Some info is downright underground.

Getting the Underground Info

When you go to an event, you want something you just can't get anywhere else. You don't want to have to hear or read the same old things, because that's just boring. What you really want is to find the kinds of knowledge that you can only get by asking specific questions. And your attendees think a lot like you do in that regard.

Gen Y is a unique group of people in that they can literally become experts on a topic's basic points in only an hour or two. When the educational system catches up to how fast these kids are, getting a degree might take four weeks instead of four years. But until then, we as event organizers can take advantage of how sharp these young turks are and let them use that sharpness for a good purpose.

One of the most useful things that will never be replaceable about going to an event is that there's time and space available to talk to knowledgeable people in a less formal capacity than normal. Going to a traditional presentation is okay, but a lot of times it's just not that interactive. And while it's not always the case, sometimes a presenter will post the same information in their talks that they've presented a dozen times before.

In this day and age it's pretty commonplace for a presenter's previous presentations to be online within days of actually happening. If your attendees are really jazzed about seeing and speaking with a particular presenter, they've already reviewed all of his or her online materials. In many cases this means they've gone to the speaker's website, YouTube and possibly trade-specific sites to devour as much info as they can straight from the presenter's mouth. But when someone is that ravenous for knowledge, there is no such thing as enough.

Millennials are notorious for being crazy about knowledge. For them, the world is a huge learning experience and classes are constantly in session. But when this knowledge reaches a capping point, like when an attendee has reviewed every possible piece of online material a presenter has put out, the only option left is to speak to that expert directly. After all, what better way to get your questions answered or to ask an opinion about something at a slightly different angle than by asking straight away?

This is something that absolutely needs to be encouraged in your attendees. This is, and will probably always be the most powerful thing we can offer at our events that you just can't get anywhere else. Sure, the Internet can give you tons of unqualified info, and if you know who to seek out you can get pretty good "basic" info. But sometimes you don't want the proverbial hamburger -- you want organic, wet-aged filet mignon. You don't get that by going to the "fast food" types of websites like YouTube.

In some cases being able to debate with your preferred experts is the best way to get the best knowledge because you can challenge them. In a video, all you can do is comment, and YouTube commenting is easy to ignore and frequently discredited by irrational people who dogmatically follow whatever their "hero" says.

Sometimes you won't get to speak to your favorite experts directly. Everyone's schedule gets complicated when an event goes on, and presenters are no different from anyone else in that regard. Even an open discussion forum won't allow you to crack every nut you want to. In these instances you have to settle for seeing and hearing your most trusted experts saying what they know in open discussion forums and debates they carry on with other people. The best thing about these kinds of forums is that you can still get great information, even if you aren't the one asking the experts questions.

No matter who does the talking, you only get the primo knowledge straight from the source.

When your attendees make a habit of coming to your events because they know they're going to be able to get the best information and even have their questions answered by people they genuinely respect, this is a great thing. First off, it benefits the attendees themselves, but it doesn't just help your credibility for creating events that bring good people together.

Remember when we touched on synergy? Synergy doesn't just happen when you have a bunch of scientists sitting in a room trying to cure cancer or create the next super weapon. It happens when a group of people who genuinely respect each other think through solving problems or creating something amazing, and it can even be "creating" something as simple as a great conversation that makes a light bulb light up in someone's head.

The kinds of deep, unbelievably informative conversations that tend to go on during major events when a revered expert and an admiring attendee meet one another tend to last until neither party has the stamina to continue onward. Those are great conversations to have, and if you've never gotten involved in such a thing I would strongly suggest you do so. If you can put your attendees into the kinds of situations where they can speak to presenters they respect that much, the amount of information that can be shared is incredible.

Of course, this doesn't just extend into an impromptu "interview" where an attendee is all but interrogating the presenter. It also means that presenter himself is learning a thing or two, if only about what to include in future talks. Sometimes a presenter doesn't realize how many things he or she knows about their topic of expertise, but that their fans would love to hear more about. Conversations of this nature take networking to a whole new level because they benefit both parties.

Networking

Naturally people come to events for the purpose of networking with one another. If not for networking, most events wouldn't be much more than lectures. The very act of connecting to other like-minded people and getting to know them a little bit better is a basic human need that we can't stress enough here.

When a group of people who respect one another communicate with a goal in mind, amazing things happen almost by accident. While it doesn't have to be something high-minded like creating the next super weapon or curing cancer, every time people network they have the chance to engage in synergy. This synergy can bring about new insights and ideas that no individual member of the group would likely have thought of on their own.

It's for this reason that events need to exist, no matter how high tech our world becomes. Not only do our attendees need face time with other people. They also need to be around people whose views they can learn and whom they can mutually help. You just never know how you might be able to help someone, or how that person in turn might be able to help you.

Being Heard

Being heard and being understood have at least one major difference between them. While being understood is the basis of giving our attendees what they want and need, it's only the base. The top of the tower involves making sure everyone's voice gets heard to the extent it needs to be. This is something we can do by allowing our attendees plenty of time and opportunities to interact, both with each other and with their favorite presenters.

A lot of times, though, being heard is just a matter of being near people who are willing to listen. Some event organizers have tested out early versions of social networking and profile creation on their websites, which has led to a more structured but still flexible method of networking. Just like with a lot of early tests, this hasn't been the most successful idea ever. However, its purpose is still the same -- allowing attendees to express their hard-won knowledge and opinions more effectively than ever before. As social networking matures further and the business world more readily accepts this form of interaction, we'll see it gaining more and more traction.

Keep in mind that almost no idea has ever had instant, widespread acceptance or success. Remember how many people have attempted to discredit Einstein's theories, and how many failures Edison had to go through before he could produce a suitable electric light bulb.

Changing How We Interact

The interactions of our atttendees are complicated, and nobody could ever manage them completely. However, as event organizers we can give our attendees every chance to interact in the ways they're most comfortable with. While millennials may spend more of their time texting their friends than talking to them in the old-fashioned way, they still need to interact with other human beings.

When it comes right down to it, how we work together hasn't changed that much over time. And when we factor in how new technologies have allowed us to connect with people all over the world, we can see all the different ways the event business has to change. If we're going to continue giving our attendees everything they need, we need to roll with the punches in a big way.

Event 3.0

6. The Influence of That on the Event Business

The event business is just like every other business in that it all comes down to what the customers want. When your attendees desire something, your options are to either bring it to them or stop doing business. While that might come across as indelicate, it's how the world works. We either have to supply what they want or go out of business trying.

As event coordinators and planners, we need to allow what our attendees want to do more than simply influence how we do business. We need to test how what we're currently providing stacks up to what our attendees are looking for, and then redesign our offerings to more effectively match those desires.

The first thing we have to do is understand our attendees and focus on helping them to understand one another. This isn't just about events, either. In order to succeed in business, we must always remember that it comes down to serving the needs of other people. Since one of the most basic human needs is to be understood, we have to literally make it our business to understand as much as we possibly can about our attendees, how they think, how they work and how they want events to go.

The next thing we have to do is help our attendees to find real expertise wherever it might be hiding. Sometimes this is simply helping them to understand that they have superior knowledge, and sometimes it's introducing them to the expert two rows up, which/whom ? they never would have seen without some help. Since expertise comes in so many shapes and sizes these days, a lot of people might not even know what to look for in the first place.

The second thing we need to do is get the people together to share more info than they can get through videos and other online sources. Since Wikipedia and YouTube can supply so much knowledge with ease and without cost, we need to step up our information sharing capabilities by a huge margin to stay ahead of the curve. A major part of this involves adapting how our businesses work so as to get the most 'underground' info into everyone's hands.

As we've hammered on for this entire book so far, networking is a non-negotiable part of the event-going experience, and it's the one part that attendees crave and can't get any other practical way. In order to make our events something that our attendees can't do without, we need to emphasize networking as much as we can, and make it as easy as humanly possible. Networking needs to take on the most active role it possibly can in our events.

Making sure our attendees are heard is also a crucial aspect of our events businesses. When we allow them to be heard and to share their knowledge, it helps us to keep our credibility and adds incredible amounts of value to their lives. While technology is a major help to this endeavor, it can't just end with using more technology. Our entire business models may need to be re-examined and sharply altered in order to make the whole thing fit together better.

How we interact with one another in every aspect of business has changed, and it will continue changing in ways we honestly can't predict. One thing we can say with absolute authority is that our businesses will grow far stronger if we work to anticipate and adapt to these different ways of interaction. If tweeting is what people do, we need to make sure we understand why, and use tweeting to our advantage. Next week they'll probably be doing something else, so this constantly adapting strategy is just beginning.

In today's world, the average worker is constantly jacked in to a variety of different networks. For these people, it's easy to find any "thing" they want, but finding people can be far different. After all, finding a person's name, address and picture is nowhere near the same as finding the actual person. Once two people find one another, it's natural to interact. However, as event organizers we need to determine the best ways to make these connections occur in the first place.

Aiding Understanding

Understanding can come about in a variety of different ways. One person can grow to understand another through reading what they've written online, by watching videos they've created and by studying any other sorts of materials the person being understood might have produced, such as podcasts and tweets.

The types of materials a person produces are often individual and based on his or her unique experiences and knowledge base. However, some things are fairly universal for nearly everyone. In this day and age, most people are on one or more of the social networking sites. Many people either tweet heavily or follow the tweets of those they respect. As well, e-mail and texting are universal parts of business in the modern world. In some ways this hyper-connectivity is a blessing to everyone involved. But in another way, it can actually lead to people hearing a lot of things but understanding very little of it.

If you've ever been told that you can't see the forest for the trees, you understand what it is to be deluged. If you spend your life absorbed in tweets, articles referred to you, e-mails that rehash things you already know, texts that consist of more filler than genuine content, and a lot of other nearly useless pieces of communication, you understand why face time is so important.

Helping people to understand one another sometimes means helping them to filter through the noise and helping shed light on the most important messages. Many virtual assistants do this successfully every day, and a deep and well connected network of support staff is something many event organizers wouldn't do business without. With a few good assistants and some ground rules, only the most precious and urgent information reaches the people it would otherwise overwhelm.

Perhaps the worst part of the information overload we all face is that it's as addictive as any drug. Even as I write this, I find myself occasionally detouring to check my e-mail, even though I know I emptied it a little while ago and I'd be informed if anything new had arrived. I check my phone for calls and texts, even though it's been sitting next to me the entire time. I have to literally turn off my wifi connection and turn off my phone to get out more than a few sentences without knee-jerk checking my different lines of connection.

Understanding comes best through face time and genuine conversation. The most recent generations have spent so much time relating to one another only through screens, some researchers have found a pronounced lack of ability to relate to each other in person. While being disconnected for a few hours might be a shock to their systems, it may be a neat way to add some "tough love" value to an event through forcing them to connect with other people in-person.

Pointing to Real Expertise

In this day and age, real experts aren't marked by how many degrees they have, or how old they are. Many of the smartest people on the planet aren't 40 years old yet, and a reasonable number aren't even 30. Because of this non-traditional age range of extraordinary insight, the entire event world has been turned on its head. We need to get away from thinking of experts as grizzled old masters who've been studying something for half a century.

After all, many of the most powerful things in our world aren't more than a few decades -- or even years -- old. How many people were tweeting in the first few years of the 21st century? None, because it didn't even exist at the time. How many people had a blog in the late 90s? There might have been a few website owners who posted regularly, but web logs are distinctly recent inventions that only became mainstream a few years ago. Because of the recent nature of these inventions and their usage, expertise may be found in high school kids instead of their grandparents.

As event organizers, we need to recognize that real expertise comes from everywhere and everyone, and make finding that expertise a central part of our events. We can use technology to do this, but the technology will change like the weather. To make real, long-lasting changes, we need to focus on thinking through where we can find expertise and then making it very obvious to every attendee where it is.

In a lot of cases, this expertise is right under our noses. Our attendees themselves are sometimes the best experts we can find, which makes what they have to say a very important part of the entire equation. When we can help our attendees to find the knowledge they themselves possess and make it easy for them to share this knowledge, we open up our events to a lot of great energy and shared insights.

Pointing to real expertise can be as simple as having open forums and debates, and it can be as sophisticated as setting up networking events in which texting a question to the speaker can change the entire speech. The level of complexity is something each individual event organizer needs to make on his or her own, but the underlying theme is that we all need to point out the best expertise we can find.

Sometimes pointing out real expertise happens on the profiles we allow attendees to place on our event websites. With properly laid out profiles, we allow our attendees to find the expertise in others coming to the event. This allows our attendees to find people who know what they're talking about and connect. Once people have connected to one another, their combined knowledge can become a sort of synergy.

When a real expert is revealed among a crowd of people, it usually comes as a surprise to everyone involved. The high-minded marketing "masters" who go around tooting their own horns constantly may have some useful knowledge, but a lot of times they're more hype than help. For the real expertise, you usually find a person in the audience who asks a really thought-provoking question that turns the discussion on its ear.

The trouble with earth-shaking questions isn't in finding them. You can't dig them up, because they happen in the moment and can't really be planned for. Great knowledge and that one magical question that uncovers it comes up when the hidden experts in the crowd all get the chance to speak their minds. This can't happen if we don't adapt to the fact that experts are literally everywhere these days.

In order to make our events into something truly special, we need to make our events as open as the Speaker Corner at London's Hyde Park. There, anyone who has something to say can simply get up and say it. I'm not suggesting we set apart a room where anyone can simply get up and speak about anything, although that might be a useful way to find experts. I'm suggesting that we make it easy for anyone who has something to add to a discussion to do so.

The method you end up using is one of the components that will either set your events apart from everyone else's or help to define an industry standard we might all follow. As sad as it is, I can't give you a 1-2-3 process by which you can make your events fool-proof and find all of the most expert attendees. There is no magic wand, and the way you choose to open up your events is as individual a decision as the clothes you wear.

One thing I can say with absolute authority is that events need to go from a presentation-centric model to a conversation-centric model. In short, we need to have conversations be the central theme of our events, instead of just letting them happen between presentations. When conversation is encouraged and assisted, a lot of great knowledge will be shared by the greatest experts in attendance.

Laying Out the underground Info

Underground info isn't found on most sites. The Internet, for all its immense complexity, is still primarily a place where people share the insights they've gained from other places. Sometimes this is real-world experience, and sometimes it's the results of thought exercises. Other times it's the kind of knowledge one can gain on one's own computer through that space between working and playing that we'll discuss later on.

The Internet is a lot like school in some ways. For example, taking classes and going to websites can expose a person to all kinds of basic information. However, getting the most in-depth and complex pieces of knowledge requires living life between websites and between classes. This kind of learning has never been very structured, but it has to take on some structure if our events are going to become better.

There was a time when people would travel to events in order to learn fairly basic information. However, those days left when the Internet made basic information available to everyone. You don't have to go to a library or call someone. All you have to do is visit an expert's website, then read a few articles and watch a few videos. One can literally become a reasonable expert on a broad topic in an hour or so, provided they're able to access the Internet and can read.

Nowadays, going to events has taken on a different type of significance altogether. Whereas people used to travel to events mostly to learn information, the worm has turned

---

so that information now takes a back seat to meeting the right people. Sometimes the people an attendee meets will eventually become business partners of some type, while other times they'll merely correspond and share knowledge with one another.

Part of pointing out knowledgable people involves allowing them to each have a space on your website, and part of it involves allowing everyone to voice their opinions during your event itself. One possible way to open up your events is to schedule shorter blocks, such as ten-minute presentations with ten-minute accompanying Q&As instead of hour-long presentations. With shorter presentations, getting to the point immediately will be paramount.

Another way to point out knowledgable people is to reduce the barriers to being a presenter. While many events require a vote by a committee for who is worthy of presenting their ideas, an event that would truly embody the concept of pointing out genuine expertise could allow the first hundred attendees who submit an online questionnaire and a brief essay to have a few minutes to speak.

Naturally, allowing almost anyone who wants to present to do so could entail some risks. But imagine the upside potential! As the old saying goes, nothing ventured is nothing gained. You might end up with primarily mediocre presentations. But if even a few turn out to be truly special, you'll be far ahead of where you'd be without ever having taken such a risk.

Creativity is the name of the game when it comes to expertise-seeking. Once you've pointed out the real experts, you need to ensure the attendees in the know meet the attendees who aren't in the know. This is the heart and soul of networking, after all.

Setting the Network Groundwork

Networking is going to happen whenever people with similar interests come into close proximity to one another. As an event organizer your best bet is to create a place where this natural networking is going to not only be allowed but encouraged. As we've discussed, part of networking involves making sure people can find one another. However, simply finding each other isn't enough. You need to make your events into fertile ground for getting people to interact with one another, as opposed to simply meeting by chance.

Some of the best ways to help people meet are to have communal break areas, parties and open forums. The more chances you give someone to ask questions and state their rebuttals, the more people will be able to connect to one another.

Generally, connections don't occur just because of having a shared interest of some kind. They tend to happen because of something interesting a person says in the moment, often without even giving it much conscious thought. Little connective moments happen in ways that no one has yet been able to predict or systematize reliably. However, these connections can grow extremely strong.

Creating open forums can take a good bit of doing. Generally, a forum needs to be moderated and guided by a third party who agrees not to express any opinions. Once this person is selected, a basic topic needs to be selected and the discussions and debates can begin. You need to strike a balance between having it be little more than a scripted play among actors and having it be a shouting match straight off of a playground.

The key to setting up a solid balance of formality and informality starts with having several levels of variously formal and less formal meetings set up. This way your events will be appealing to more formal and traditional types of people as well as more free-wheeling types. There are two very different groups being represented at every event, after all: those who value the structure of the event and those who want their freedom more than anything else.

The structure-loving people are the ones who want an organized place to meet and listen to presenters. Their love of formality makes them want experts who have some sort of official social proof. Without the folks who love structure, most of our world would be chaotic and ruled by whimsy. Of course, their ways can seem a little dry and boring to people who love to be thrilled and surprised a lot.

On the other hand, there are those who shun structure whenever they can. These are the folks who love a good adventure and live for the next random moment of inspiration. While not all of these people are entrepreneurs, they are more likely to jump out of the restrictions of the corporate world and build their own businesses. If they're employees, you'll find them working in startups. What you won't find them doing very often is sitting in lengthy presentations playing stenographer. This type of person is very common among the younger generations, and they get what's being said very quickly.

Your events need to have some presentations put on by widely respected experts, or you won't do much to impress the more structure-hungry types of attendees. These do well to draw them in, but everybody needs to cut loose to some extent. Once they're in your events, they might find it interesting to try more open-ended forums and discussion groups. Since they're also out to network, they'll most likely grow to appreciate the opportunities for conversation afforded them by forums of this nature.

On the other hand, structure-haters will more likely roll their eyes if they think there's nothing but what they would call "a bunch of lectures" at your events. This is a group that often shunned formal education, after all. To them, a place where they can discuss a topic is worth far more than a place where they can just hear about it from someone who won't answer their more in-depth and specific questions. This is a group that wants to interact above all else.

Really Listening

Genuine listening is one of the most important parts of any interaction, including that between attendees at one of your events. While you might think this is the same as being heard, it isn't. This is about doing more than just facilitating communication between attendees. We need to redefine our events so they'll allow people to listen to one another and not just talk at others in a constant stream of noise.

In our world, noise is everywhere, and not just the noises of city life. In a world where tweets, e-mails, instant messages and notifications of every sort bombard us all, it's hard to really listen to anything. Some people say that today's youngest generations have attention deficit disorder, and it's true. But it isn't really a disorder anymore, but it is an adaptation to a world where no one has the time to really focus on most things.

In order to get people to really listen to each other, you have to allow them to speak for more than five seconds at a time. While most of the world is busy scurrying around trying to do several things at one time, it may actually be necessary to slow down the pacing of your events slightly, and allow more time to do certain things. The event industry has been so concerned with doing more within the same amount of time, but sometimes hurrying actually allows less useful actions to take place.

It may seem strange that scheduling less structured presentations and other more formal happenings within your events could be a positive step toward getting more done. When you've attracted both pro-structure and anti-structure people, you can let their different temperaments play off of one another and make your events even better places to network.

When you provide enough structure for comfort, you allow people to let down some of their guard. After all, you want them to know why they've come to your events in the first place. You could even set up a section to be a sort of "corral" your attendees could use as an open, sandbox-like meeting place.

In this world, people are very open to sharing. In the next chapter we'll discuss how too much sharing can be a serious problem.

7. The Dangers of Excessive Sharing...

In our world, most people share to excess. The most recent generations are extremely comfortable, both in their own skins and in the world. Millennials are renowned for being extremely sure of themselves, especially when it comes to social networking. There isn't much they aren't willing to share.

Sharing starts the first time someone wants to be seen by members of their peer group. For millennials this began when they hit their teen years, and it started even earlier in life for later generations. This sharing extends to everything they do, and there is little that happens in their lives that doesn't immediately get shared in some fashion.

Remember that this is an era when texts and tweets are the way things get said. If it can't be expressed in 140 characters or less, most people don't say it in the first place unless they're blogging. Now, you can allow technology to make your events obsolete, or you can make it into your ally. It isn't always going to be easy, but with effort you can make it work.

Since technophobia is dead, you can't just assume that people aren't online or aren't connecting to one another this way. People network in a wide variety of different ways every day, and they'll continue to do so also in the future. Connecting to other people is what the most recent generations do best.

Fortunately, we can make this technology work to strengthen our events. We can generate a buzz using the very technology that people all around us are already using, instead of allowing it to distract and pull them away from our events. If we aren't proactive, we're going to be left behind. Sharing is great, but sometimes it gets to be too much. We can't stop it, so we need to channel it for our own purposes.

Technology Turning Against Us

Today's technologies are more connected than ever before. Social networking is one of the most powerful media in the world nowadays. When a person has something on their mind, they put it on their status message first and do anything else second. Ask anybody under 30 and you'll get that confirmed.

The nature of social networking is that people on social networks know a lot about one another. They share everything that happens in their lives, including what they're doing professionally. So if someone is going to one of your events, they're going to share it everywhere they frequent.

Today the primary social networking platforms are Twitter, LinkedIn and Facebook, but soon enough they'll change to something else. The important part for us is to remain on the cutting edge of how our attendees communicate. When they use social networking to share where they're going, we want to be sure we're being shared in the best possible light.

Which do you want to be? The event their boss is making them go to, or the event they can't wait to go to? We've already talked about giving them what they want and how we need to change our ways to maximize this giving. Now we need to talk about making technology help us to help as many attendees as humanly possible.

It starts out with the litttle things like adding small icons to our advertisements like "Follow us on Twitter" and the like. These days everyone has those buttons, and people actually click them. Getting a high ranking on Digg can actually make a serious difference, both in your attendance and in the satisfaction of your attendees.

Social networking websites can help us in a variety of different ways. They can help our events be noticed by prospective attendees, they can keep us fresh in people's minds in between events, and they can even generate a buzz when we institute a new event. Social networking websites can be the best things to happen to our events, especially when they're shared as readily as people today like to share things.

Being Lost in the Shuffle

If you ask 100 people what the first thing they do is when they get online, at least half will say they check their social networks. There's always something happening, and most people have to be sure they're not missing out on anything good. If there's nothing special going on, it's no big deal. But if most people put the kind of vigilance into everything else that they put into their social networks, they'd be downright paranoid.

We can use this hyper-vigilance to our advantage in promoting our events. If you don't have all the popular types of accounts, they're easy enough to set up. When you have an event coming up, you naturally move it to the top of the list and promote it like crazy. You also want to make sure you're getting close to your attendees and potential attendees. After all, there are only so many degrees of separation between people these days.

A major part of being noticed resides in allowing a network to work for you. When one person signs up for your event, even if it's just for information, you have access to their network. While your own personal ethics will dictate how vigorously you pursue these newly-acquired leads, it never hurts to let them know your events exist. Plus, in between your events, you can make sure your past attendees don't forget about you.

Loosing Our Edge

Nobody wants to go stale, and going stale in the online sense means not regularly updating your status and not offering something of value on an equally regular basis. When you update regularly and keep yourself in your attendees' consciousness, you stay fresh and your events stay well-attended.

The best ways to stay fresh are to keep up your social networking accounts and to make sure you send out occasional messages to the people connected to your profile. Remember that these need to be high-value information, not just advertisements. Today's young people are very good at telling the difference between the two and filtering out the latter.

Great leads are actual attendees who pay to go to your events. Just like with every other kind of customers, attendees are good when they may buy and great when they actually do. Sometimes a potential attendee is sitting on the proverbial fence, but after a long enough time it's okay to release someone from the list. Sometimes the trick to keeping someone who may or may not pull the trigger is to create a buzz around your event.

Falling Asleep

Entrepreneurs are well known for wanting to create a buzz. In some cases creating a buzz is more successful than in others, but it generally means something important is happening. In the case of an event, having a buzz surrounding it is a powerful way to get people excited. This excitement is most easily stirred up by making mention of it in gradually more amped-up terms on your social networking channels.

Social networking is the best way short of a blimp to get a buzz going for an event. When you release plenty of solid information all the time and follow it up with a great pitch, everyone will know you offer tons of value at your events. Rather like you should never dig a well when you're thirsty, trying to start out generating a buzz when your event is near is too late.

Of course, this is why you're reading this now. If you haven't built your online networking profiles yet, do so immediately. Then connect with your future attendees. Greet them as friends and colleagues and treat them with candor, and they'll believe you when you say you're excited about your next event.

Another great thing about being genuinely involved with your event's social network is that when you post something your'e excited about, they'll also get excited about it. When they get excited, they're certain to share it. While some people hate sharing, especially when it comes to things like games and music, online sharing has been shown to be very helpful to those who produce what gets shared.

Technology Can Help Or Hurt Us

Having your event be shared may not sound good to start with, but it has a lot of benefits to it. For starters, you get more attendees. For another thing, you get more

---

excitement because group commitments tend to be stronger than individual ones. Thirdly, you get people to feel a sense of ownership over your events. This feeling of ownership can be very powerful and can lead to die-hard attendees who contribute a lot to your events.

We've talked about how anyone and everyone can be an expert these days. The great thing about being close with your network is that you'll attract a reasonably high percentage of people who are close to the other people in their networks. Through these connections you'll receive even more attendees who will be led to respect your events.

Through group polarization, when you have a lot of friends and colleagues who believe something, the group tends to reinforce this belief among its members. This nearly Orwellian groupthink can be used very productively when you want to make your events stand out, both from the crowd and among the crowd.

However, there's the ineffective way to go -- "targetting" everyone -- and then there's being more precise in who you really go after. You don't want to be thought of as a spammer, and you want to use your energy to its utmost advantage. Let's look at the better way to target great customers versus the way far too many misinformed event organizers go about it.

Ready, Fire, Aim

Being connected to every kind of social networking platform is all well and good, but it's just the first step toward

---

becoming an online powerhouse in the event industry. You also want to take it further than just talking at people and constantly telling them this and that. While what you offer might be incredibly valuable and insightful, there's a sad but established trend online -- a lot of people would rather listen than speak.

Granted, there's nothing wrong with people who choose to take in the knowledge being presented to them. But having a massive list of people who do that, and only that, can seriously weigh down your efforts to successfully market your events. It sounds like the more people you have in your network, the better off you are. Indeed, a lot of event organizers will actually brag about having thousands of followers and friends online. The problem is, this number can actually be more harm than help.

When you start out into social networking, you have to practice "ready, fire, aim." This means you send out something, then refine it as time goes on. This way you can get an increasingly good feel for how well your marketing efforts are being received, and who is receiving them the best. However, simply piling up a huge list of contacts can be counterproductive if most of them just listen and never respond.

The trouble with your contact lists is that they're visible to everyone, including your competitors. So while you're busy hammering away and sending out all kinds of interesting, well researched and brilliantly written materials, your competitor can do the same thing -- to your list. So all the work you've done to generate leads will be helping him at least as much as it helps you, and possibly moreso.

The best way to engage your most active members is to work with them only. You need to actually move away from talking much to the people who don't respond and don't share what you have to say. If they don't share you with their friends, your network won't grow organically. Since organic growth is what you want in an online following, forget the folks who just passively let what you send wash over them. Focus instead on the people who really matter -- the folks who like, Digg, and otherwise recommend and boost your efforts.

Great attendees are a lot like any other kind of great customers. They not only pay you, but recommend you to others who are likely to pay you, as well. The process of having an ever-growing group of people who refer you to others who in turn refer you is known as "going viral," .

There are a number of ways you can speak to only your active members, including our own Social Hurricane. This service allows you to reach out only to your active members, instead of sending blanket messages to everyone and exposing your customers to your competition.

Now that we've covered the changes taking place in the event industry, we need to discuss what this little caterpillar is likely going to turn into. The newest generations want things their parents and grandparents never could have imagined, and in Chapter 8 we're going to say precisely what kind of event that is. Remember that events are about both business and fun.

8. Embracing the New Business and Fun Framework

The modern way to run events is to mix business and fun together. The happiest and most financially successful people in the world are generally part of the same group, after all. Some would even say that happiness and wealth blend together marvelously. Passion and profit are sometimes one and the same, and we need to keep that in mind in our events. Through having less formality, we need to make our events something that opens the floor for an enjoyable experience.

We've touched on this throughout the book and it bears repeating -- events need to be fun enough to capture and hold the attention of the modern worker. Your events need to rip them from their constant attachment to technology long enough to take in great information and meet great people.

The Mixture of Business and Fun

Only a truly sad individual would think that business has to be dry and boring. Even in the oldest days of the event industry, good organizers kept things a little loose and spritely when it was possible. Of course, with traditionalists it was easy to simply funnel people wherever you wanted them to go and make them work with your methods. Millennials are a lot different.

Today's attendees are as fun-loving as you'll ever find. For them, an event's success is measurable by the network and the knowledge they gain. But measurements aren't everything. There's also the matter of whether an event was fun or not. Who would go to something where they're bored out of their mind? Not many people.

Through the use of open forums, panels with experts and open stages, you can allow everyone to speak, be heard and meet people. But aside from all of the rational reasons why these are great ideas, you'll also give your attendees a great time. Keep things mixed up a bit and let some spontaneity happen, and your events will be known for more than just being great places to network and learn. They'll be known for a good time, and not much can beat that.

What Events Should Be

An event should be broken down into sections that correspond to how people today want to work. For contrast's sake, we should take a brief look at how events typically look today. The standard issue event looks essentially like this:

- Morning keynote session or sessions, outlining the relevant topics in broader terms

- Networking/coffee break

- Parallel sessions to delve deeper into general topics covered in the keynote(s)

- Closing session

During a typical event, breaks are sporadic throughout the day. The relevance of these breaks is that they are the only traditional time where networking takes place. As a general rule, people are either involved in a lecture on a topic or moving from one lecture to another. Breaks interrupt the monotony and give people a chance to move around, but they're far too short to have deep and meaningful conversations.

In order to enable the kinds of interactions we've been talking about throughout this book, an entirely different tack needs to be taken. The purpose of the keynote is to attract people by having a big name person speak, but after that the process needs to become a bit less formal. One-way presentations are efficient, but they lack the customization you can only get in person. After this, the event should break up into three equally important tracks: the Networking track, the Open stage/Chance2speak track and the Structured formal content track. Finally, the close of an event should be a gathering resembling a party, to really solidify the connections people have made during the event itself. Let's elaborate on the tracks first.

The Networking Track

Networking is a cornerstone of an event, and plenty of networking opportunities should be offered throughout the days of every event. Through allowing people to mingle in a stress-free environment where they aren't rushing from one thing to the next, we can give a lot of the younger generation workers what they want the most -- genuine connections. These connections, in turn, will allow these attendees to get to know the people they're meeting. They'll also get to meet more than just the people they randomly bump into in passing.

Building a network starts with meeting someone. Sometimes you'll notice something you both have in common, and sometimes it starts with a random shot in the dark. Either way, a conversation develops that can literally change lives. By having a track of different meetings designed specifically for networking, we're legitimizing what people have desperately wanted to do for years but haven't had the chance to do.

When we not only allow but encourage our attendees to network, we build the type of connections that are extremely valuable to both them and us. When attendees network as a major part of the event, they carry that networking outward and become boosters for our events. The type of person who really wants to network embodies all of the qualities of a sales person: they're generally outgoing, positive, and really want to meet people. When the networkers leave an event they love, they're going to become the best possible free advertisers.

You can't buy marketing like highly satisfied attendees who love to share what they've been up to. Since this type of person most likely already has a large and vibrant network, this track is going to result in unbelievable profit opportunities through additional lead generation. Since these leads will be warmed up through their existing relationships with your attendees, they'll have an above-average conversion rate.

Remember that your objective here won't be to keep your networking track as a "hidden gem" to be discovered when an attendee gets to your event. It'll be one of the four main draws, which include the keynote speaker(s) and the other two tracks. Also keep in mind that in this type of event, going along one track won't confine an attendee to only doing those components. Starting out on the networking track won't squeeze out the other two tracks, and mixing of all three should be very common. Now that we've covered networking, let's talk about how the open stage will change the way people meet at events.

The Open Stage Track

An open stage is a tempting place to say what's on your mind. While not every idea is going to be ground-breaking, sometimes the worst idea is still pretty good. Professional events don't typically attract the rants people feel free to do in their blogs, so 99% of the content you have on an open stage is the best ideas people have. In a lot of cases, you'll get people offering services and ideas that can add tremendous value to a lot of their listeners. Another interesting thing your stages are bound to attract are great listeners who are in the

---

market for what the speakers are hawking, both in regard to product/service offerings and ideas being broached.

Great ideas can be worth billions of dollars to the right people, and the next billion-dollar idea could be sitting in someone's head right next to you. If that person never says a word, and they've got the perfect peanut butter for your jelly, imagine the amazing potential that could be lost forever. Can you imagine if the next generation of great entrepreneurs had easy access to potential partners speaking right in front of them? Imagine if Apple founders Jobs and Wozniak had had such a ready-made place to connect, instead of having to meet by chance. Imagine if the Google guys Page and Brin had been able to meet this efficiently.

Untold numbers of entrepreneurial pairings could be found along this open stage track. When you combine this with the networking track, you get a one-two combo that can't be beaten for meeting other like-minded, hungry people. This hunger can be applied to a huge number of potential ventures. Even if two future Forbes list members don't end up meeting at the event, the open stage can still stimulate a lot of important discussions.

One of the unfortunate things about this or any other book is that no one in the world knows precisely where the future is going to take us. When I was in high school, no kid had a cell phone. Nowadays you'd have to hunt around to find anyone under 10 who doesn't have one. They're considered essential. I remember what tapes are, and could rattle off a list of bands today's kids have probably never heard of. The point isn't to say how I'm an old man who should probably be sitting in a rocking chair, but to express that the way and speed at which the world is changing makes total predictions impossible. But someone has an idea.

That idea person might very well be attending your events, and you wouldn't even know the brilliance hidden inside them. In some cases, such a visionary might not even realize that what they're thinking of could change the world as thoroughly as the Internet has. This person is waiting to be heard and have his or her ideas discovered, and the open stage track is among the best possible places to make this happen.

When a person can sign up, go up and speak for a few minutes, no one knows a day in advance what the person is going to be talking about. It could be nothing of interest, or it could absolutely blow people away. I'm extremely excited about the hidden treasures that will be revealed when more event organizers begin structuring their events this way, because the amount of ideas that will be shared may multiply by a factor of 100.

Now let's bring it home with a discussion of why formal content is still important.

The Formal Content Track

Formal content has been over-emphasized in the event industry for a very long time. Because of this fact, in this book I've been extremely hesitant to talk about how important formal content remains to this day. Having speakers make formal presentations is important because of the information they have to share that they can't squeeze into brief videos, and because some attendees continue to come to events to learn information gleaned from other people's experiences. As important as networking and experiencing new ideas are, formal content from well-known experts is still a solid tool in every attendee's toolbox.

Formal content is what keeps any industry somewhat orderly, and allows its members to have standards they can fall back to when their own experiences wouldn't give them enough insight to make a decision. If you've ever attended a great presentation, you've left charged with energy, ideas you've jotted down for later, and a deeper understanding of the subject matter than you had before.

Granted, you can get a solid understanding of most things through a book or Wikipedia article. But there's nothing like hearing an expert explain in their own words what a concept really means. To be around a person who really cares about a subject is far different than reading dry, emotionless words from a page or a screen.

The content of your events is a key draw to a lot of more traditionally-minded attendees, as well. While the party at the end of the event and the networking are sure draws that offer obvious advantages, some people just aren't that sociable. To them, an event still needs to have an element of listening and learning through presentations in order to remain legitimate. As important as the other tracks are, the structured and formal track has as much of a place as it always has in keeping your events from becoming too informal.

Ultimately, the structure of your event is your decision. No one else can tell you how to run your events, though the ideas in this book have been intended to advise you on where the industry is likely heading. Naturally, technology plays a role, but that role is always second to the structure of the event itself. Having ample choices with a wide range of interactivity is the ultimate way to work with how the youngest generations think and attend.

Parting Words

This entire book has been dedicated to saying one thing in a dozen different ways. If our events are going to stand the test of time and actually grow stronger with the changing world, we're going to need to radically alter the way we look at them. Not only are we going to have to fix up the way we use technology. We also need to rethink the way we see our events as what they are now and what they can be, as opposed to what they have been in the past.

Events used to be about disseminating information, but times have changed. Since we can find whatever we like online, the need for that in person is largely gone. What we need now is to share deeper insights which can only be shared between individual people having actual conversations. Networking is the major purpose of today's events, whether it's obvious to us or not.

Today's people are more networked than ever before, and we have to pay attention to this. More importantly, we have to use this desire and power to network as a means of making our events better, as opposed to just using it as an excuse to fail. Our success depends on our ability to adapt to how our attendees want their events to go, and just as importantly who they want to meet.

We can help them do these things through technology, but technology is primarily just a part of "how." It's never much of "why" we need to do this. So long as we keep technology under control and serving us, our events will grow stronger. If we don't, technology could leave us searching for new professions.

Thank you for reading this, and I hope you've gotten some great lessons out of it. Of course, for the very best lessons you'll have to catch me at an event.

Cool ideas I just thought of...

_____

_____

_____

_____

_____

_____

_____

_____

_____

_____

_____

_____